The Order for th...
Holy Commu...
also called
The Eucharist
and
The Lord's Supper

C000231683

HOLY TRINITY. ECCLESHALL

Order Two

Church House Publishing

Published by   Church House Publishing
                    Church House
                    Great Smith Street
                    London SW1P 3NZ

Copyright ©   *The Archbishops' Council 2000*

                    First published 2000

                    0 7151 2027 1

Printed and bound by ArklePrint Ltd, Northampton on 80 gsm Dutchman Ivory

Typeset in Gill Sans by John Morgan and Shirley Thompson/Omnific Designed by Derek Birdsall RDI

The material in this booklet is extracted from *Common Worship: Services and Prayers for the Church of England*. It comprises:

¶ The Order for the Celebration of Holy Communion: Order Two;

¶ extract from Prayers for Various Occasions;

¶ extracts from Notes to Holy Communion;

¶ General Rules.

For other material, page references to *Common Worship: Services and Prayers for the Church of England* are supplied.

Pagination   This booklet has two sets of page numbers. The outer numbers are the booklet's own page numbers, while the inner numbers near the centre of most pages refer to the equivalent pages in *Common Worship: Services and Prayers for the Church of England*.

Contents

iv   General Notes

     Order Two

vi   Structure

I   **Order Two**

17   Annex to Order Two
      Third Exhortation from *The Book of Common Prayer*   17
      Proper Prefaces from *The Book of Common Prayer*   18

19   A Collect for the Queen

20   **Notes**

25   **General Rules for Regulating Authorized Forms of Service**

26   Authorization

26   Acknowledgements

¶ General Notes

¶ Preparation

Careful devotional preparation before the service is recommended for every communicant. A Form of Preparation for public or private use is provided (page 161 in *Common Worship: Services and Prayers for the Church of England*).

¶ Ministries

Holy Communion is celebrated by the whole people of God gathered for worship. The ministry of the members of the congregation is expressed through their active participation together in the words and actions of the service, but also by some of them reading the Scripture passages, leading the prayers of intercession, and, if authorized, assisting with the distribution of communion.

In some traditions the ministry of the deacon at Holy Communion has included some of the following elements: the bringing in of the Book of the Gospels, the invitation to confession, the reading of the Gospel, the preaching of the sermon when licensed to do so, a part in the prayers of intercession, the preparation of the table and the gifts, a part in the distribution, the ablutions and the dismissal.

The deacon's liturgical ministry provides an appropriate model for the ministry of an assisting priest, a Reader, or another episcopally authorized minister in a leadership ministry that complements that of the president.

The unity of the liturgy is served by the ministry of the president, who in presiding over the whole service holds word and sacrament together and draws the congregation into a worshipping community.

The president at Holy Communion (who, in accordance with the provisions of Canon B 12 'Of the Ministry of the Holy Communion', must have been episcopally ordained priest) expresses this ministry by saying the opening Greeting, the Absolution, the Collect, the Peace and the Blessing. The president must say the Eucharistic Prayer, break the consecrated bread and receive the sacrament on every occasion. When appropriate, the president may, after greeting the people, delegate the leadership of all or parts of the Gathering and the Liturgy of the Word to a deacon, Reader or other authorized lay person.

In the absence of a priest for the first part of the service, a deacon, Reader or other authorized lay person may lead the entire Gathering and Liturgy of the Word.

When the bishop is present, he normally presides over the whole service.

As provided in Canon B 18 the sermon shall be preached by a duly authorized minister, deaconess, Reader or lay worker or, at the invitation of the minister having the cure of souls and with the permission of the bishop, another person.

¶   Communicant members of other Churches

Baptized persons who are communicant members of other Churches which subscribe to the doctrine of the Holy Trinity and are in good standing in their own Church shall be admitted to Communion in accordance with Canon B 15A.

In preparing for the service, the priest should consult the complete provision in Common Worship: Services and Prayers for the Church of England (pages 155–335).

For further Notes, see pages 20–24.

The people and the priest

¶ prepare for worship

¶ hear and respond to the commandments of God

¶ keep silence and pray a Collect

¶ proclaim and respond to the word of God

¶ prepare the table

¶ pray for the Church and the world

¶ confess their sins and are assured of God's forgiveness

¶ praise God for his goodness

¶ pray the Consecration Prayer

¶ receive communion

¶ respond with thanksgiving

¶ depart with God's blessing

For Notes, see pages iv–v and 20–24.

Order Two

A hymn may be sung.

The Lord's Prayer

Our Father, which art in heaven,
hallowed be thy name;
thy kingdom come;
thy will be done,
in earth as it is in heaven.
Give us this day our daily bread.
And forgive us our trespasses,
as we forgive them that trespass against us.
And lead us not into temptation;
but deliver us from evil. Amen.

Prayer of Preparation

Almighty God,
unto whom all hearts be open,
all desires known,
and from whom no secrets are hid:
cleanse the thoughts of our hearts
by the inspiration of thy Holy Spirit,
that we may perfectly love thee,
and worthily magnify thy holy name;
through Christ our Lord.

All **Amen.**

The Commandments

*The priest reads the Ten Commandments and the people make
the response. Or, except on the first Sundays of Advent and Lent,
the Summary of the Law or Kyrie eleison may be used.*

God spake these words and said:
I am the Lord thy God; thou shalt have none other gods but me.

All **Lord, have mercy upon us,
and incline our hearts to keep this law.**

Thou shalt not make to thyself any graven image,
nor the likeness of any thing that is in heaven above,
or in the earth beneath, or in the water under the earth.
Thou shalt not bow down to them, nor worship them:
for I the Lord thy God am a jealous God,
and visit the sins of the fathers upon the children
    unto the third and fourth generation of them that hate me,
and shew mercy unto thousands in them that love me
    and keep my commandments.

All **Lord, have mercy upon us,
and incline our hearts to keep this law.**

Thou shalt not take the name of the Lord thy God in vain:
for the Lord will not hold him guiltless that taketh his name in vain.

All **Lord, have mercy upon us,
and incline our hearts to keep this law.**

Remember that thou keep holy the Sabbath day.
Six days shalt thou labour, and do all that thou hast to do;
but the seventh day is the Sabbath of the Lord thy God.
In it thou shalt do no manner of work,
thou, and thy son, and thy daughter,
thy manservant, and thy maidservant,
thy cattle, and the stranger that is within thy gates.
For in six days the Lord made heaven and earth,
the sea, and all that in them is,
and rested the seventh day:
wherefore the Lord blessed the seventh day, and hallowed it.

All **Lord, have mercy upon us,
and incline our hearts to keep this law.**

Honour thy father and thy mother;
that thy days may be long in the land
   which the Lord thy God giveth thee.

All **Lord, have mercy upon us,
and incline our hearts to keep this law.**

Thou shalt do no murder.

All **Lord, have mercy upon us,
and incline our hearts to keep this law.**

Thou shalt not commit adultery.

All **Lord, have mercy upon us,
and incline our hearts to keep this law.**

Thou shalt not steal.

All **Lord, have mercy upon us,
and incline our hearts to keep this law.**

Thou shalt not bear false witness against thy neighbour.

All **Lord, have mercy upon us,
and incline our hearts to keep this law.**

Thou shalt not covet thy neighbour's house,
thou shalt not covet thy neighbour's wife, nor his servant,
nor his maid, nor his ox, nor his ass, nor anything that is his.

All **Lord, have mercy upon us,
and write all these thy laws in our hearts, we beseech thee.**

Or this Summary of the Law may be said

Our Lord Jesus Christ said:
Hear, O Israel, the Lord our God is one Lord;
and thou shalt love the Lord thy God with all thy heart,
and with all thy soul, and with all thy mind,
and with all thy strength.
This is the first commandment.

And the second is like, namely this:
Thou shalt love thy neighbour as thyself.
There is none other commandment greater than these.
On these two commandments hang all the law
   and the prophets.

All **Lord, have mercy upon us,
and write all these thy laws in our hearts,
   we beseech thee.**

Lord, have mercy.
All **Lord, have mercy.**
Lord, have mercy.

All **Christ, have mercy.**
Christ, have mercy.
All **Christ, have mercy.**

Lord, have mercy.
All **Lord, have mercy.**
Lord, have mercy.

(or)

Kyrie, eleison.
All **Kyrie, eleison**.
Kyrie, eleison.

All **Christe, eleison.**
Christe, eleison.
All **Christe, eleison.**

Kyrie, eleison.
All **Kyrie, eleison**.
Kyrie, eleison.

The Collect for the Sovereign may be said

Almighty God, whose kingdom is everlasting, and power infinite:
have mercy upon the whole Church; and so rule the heart of
thy chosen servant *Elizabeth*, *our Queen* and Governor, that she
(knowing whose minister she is) may above all things seek thy
honour and glory: and that we and all her subjects (duly considering
whose authority she hath) may faithfully serve, honour and humbly
obey her, in thee, and for thee, according to thy blessed word and
ordinance; through Jesus Christ our Lord, who with thee and the
Holy Ghost liveth and reigneth, ever one God, world without end.
All **Amen.**

The Collect

The priest may say

The Lord be with you
All   **and with thy spirit.**
Let us pray.

The priest says the Collect of the Day.

Epistle

*A Lesson from the Old Testament may be read
and a Psalm may be used.*

The reader says

The Lesson is written in the … chapter of …
beginning at the … verse.

At the end

Here endeth the Lesson.

The reader says

The Epistle is written in the … chapter of …
beginning at the … verse.

At the end

Here endeth the Epistle.

A hymn may be sung.

Gospel

The reader says

The holy Gospel is written in the … chapter of the Gospel
according to Saint …, beginning at the … verse.

All may respond

All   **Glory be to thee, O Lord.**

At the end the reader may say

This is the Gospel of the Lord.

All may respond

All   **Praise be to thee, O Christ.**

The Creed

The Creed is used on every Sunday and Holy Day
and may be used on other days also.

All　**I believe in one God the Father almighty,**
maker of heaven and earth,
and of all things
visible and invisible:

And in one Lord Jesus Christ,
the only-begotten Son of God,
begotten of his Father before all worlds,
God of God, Light of Light,
very God of very God,
begotten, not made,
being of one substance with the Father,
by whom all things were made;
who for us men and for our salvation
came down from heaven,
and was incarnate by the Holy Ghost of the Virgin Mary,
and was made man,
and was crucified also for us under Pontius Pilate.
He suffered and was buried,
and the third day he rose again
according to the Scriptures,
and ascended into heaven,
and sitteth on the right hand of the Father.
And he shall come again with glory
to judge both the quick and the dead:
whose kingdom shall have no end.

And I believe in the Holy Ghost,
the Lord and giver of life,
who proceedeth from the Father and the Son,
who with the Father and the Son together
is worshipped and glorified,
who spake by the prophets.
And I believe one catholic and apostolic Church.
I acknowledge one baptism for the remission of sins.
And I look for the resurrection of the dead,
and the life of the world to come.
Amen.

Banns of marriage may be published and notices given.

Sermon

Offertory

One of the following or another sentence of Scripture is used

Let your light so shine before men, that they may see your good works, and glorify your Father which is in heaven.   *Matthew 5.16*

Lay not up for yourselves treasure upon the earth; where the rust and moth doth corrupt, and where thieves break through and steal: but lay up for yourselves treasures in heaven; where neither rust nor moth doth corrupt, and where thieves do not break through and steal.
Matthew 6.19

All things come of thee, and of thine own do we give thee.
1 Chronicles 29.14

Whoso hath this world's good, and seeth his brother have need, and shutteth up his compassion from him, how dwelleth the love of God in him?   *1 John 3.17*

A hymn may be sung.

The gifts of the people may be gathered and presented.

The priest places the bread and wine upon the table.

Intercession

Brief biddings may be given.

Let us pray for the whole state of Christ's Church militant here
in earth.

Almighty and ever-living God, who by thy holy apostle hast taught
us to make prayers and supplications, and to give thanks, for all men:
we humbly beseech thee most mercifully [to accept our alms and
oblations, and] to receive these our prayers, which we offer unto thy
divine majesty; beseeching thee to inspire continually the universal
Church with the spirit of truth, unity, and concord: and grant, that
all they that do confess thy holy name may agree in the truth of thy
holy word, and live in unity and godly love.

We beseech thee also to save and defend all Christian kings, princes
and governors; and specially thy servant *Elizabeth our Queen*, that
under her we may be godly and quietly governed: and grant unto her
whole Council, and to all that are put in authority under her, that
they may truly and impartially minister justice, to the punishment
of wickedness and vice, and to the maintenance of thy true religion
and virtue.

Give grace, O heavenly Father, to all bishops, priests and deacons,
that they may both by their life and doctrine set forth thy true
and lively word, and rightly and duly administer thy holy sacraments:
and to all thy people give thy heavenly grace; and specially to this
congregation here present; that, with meek heart and due
reverence, they may hear and receive thy holy word; truly serving
thee in holiness and righteousness all the days of their life.

And we most humbly beseech thee of thy goodness, O Lord,
to comfort and succour all them, who in this transitory life are
in trouble, sorrow, need, sickness, or any other adversity.

And we also bless thy holy name for all thy servants departed this
life in thy faith and fear; beseeching thee to give us grace so to
follow their good examples, that with them we may be partakers
of thy heavenly kingdom.

Grant this, O Father, for Jesus Christ's sake, our only mediator
and advocate.

All **Amen.**

The priest may read the Exhortation (page 17) or one of the other Exhortations in The Book of Common Prayer.

Invitation to Confession

Ye that do truly and earnestly repent you of your sins, and are in love and charity with your neighbours, and intend to lead a new life, following the commandments of God, and walking from henceforth in his holy ways: draw near with faith, and take this holy sacrament to your comfort; and make your humble confession to almighty God, meekly kneeling upon your knees.

Confession

All **Almighty God,**
Father of our Lord Jesus Christ,
maker of all things, judge of all men:
we acknowledge and bewail
    our manifold sins and wickedness,
which we, from time to time,
    most grievously have committed,
by thought, word and deed,
against thy divine majesty,
provoking most justly thy wrath and indignation against us.
We do earnestly repent,
and are heartily sorry for these our misdoings;
the remembrance of them is grievous unto us;
the burden of them is intolerable.
Have mercy upon us,
have mercy upon us, most merciful Father;
for thy Son our Lord Jesus Christ's sake,
forgive us all that is past;
and grant that we may ever hereafter
serve and please thee in newness of life,
to the honour and glory of thy name;
through Jesus Christ our Lord.
Amen.

Absolution

The priest says

Almighty God, our heavenly Father,
who of his great mercy
hath promised forgiveness of sins
to all them that with hearty repentance and true faith
    turn unto him:
have mercy upon *you*;
pardon and deliver *you* from all *your* sins;
confirm and strengthen *you* in all goodness;
and bring *you* to everlasting life;
through Jesus Christ our Lord.

All   **Amen.**

The Comfortable Words

Hear what comfortable words our Saviour Christ saith
unto all that truly turn to him:

Come unto me, all that travail and are heavy laden,
and I will refresh you.   *Matthew 11.28*

So God loved the world, that he gave his only-begotten Son,
to the end that all that believe in him should not perish,
but have everlasting life.   *John 3.16*

Hear also what Saint Paul saith:
This is a true saying, and worthy of all men to be received,
that Christ Jesus came into the world to save sinners. *1 Timothy 1.15*

Hear also what Saint John saith:
If any man sin, we have an advocate with the Father,
Jesus Christ the righteous;
and he is the propitiation for our sins.   *1 John 2.1,2*

Preface

The priest and the people praise God for his goodness.

The Lord be with you
All **and with thy spirit.**

Lift up your hearts.
All **We lift them up unto the Lord.**

Let us give thanks unto our Lord God.
All **It is meet and right so to do.**

The priest says

It is very meet, right and our bounden duty,
that we should at all times, and in all places, give thanks unto thee,
O Lord, holy Father,
almighty, everlasting God.

A Proper Preface may follow (see Note 28).

Therefore with angels and archangels,
and with all the company of heaven,
we laud and magnify thy glorious name,
evermore praising thee, and *saying*:

All **Holy, holy, holy, Lord God of hosts,
heaven and earth are full of thy glory.
Glory be to thee, O Lord most high.
[Amen.]**

These words may also be used

All **Blessed is he that cometh in the name of the Lord.
Hosanna in the highest.**

Prayer of Humble Access

We do not presume
to come to this thy table, O merciful Lord,
trusting in our own righteousness,
but in thy manifold and great mercies.
We are not worthy
so much as to gather up the crumbs under thy table.
But thou art the same Lord,
whose property is always to have mercy:
grant us therefore, gracious Lord,
so to eat the flesh of thy dear Son Jesus Christ,
and to drink his blood,
that our sinful bodies may be made clean by his body,
and our souls washed through his most precious blood,
and that we may evermore dwell in him, and he in us.

All **Amen.**

The Prayer of Consecration

The priest, standing at the table, says the Prayer of Consecration

Almighty God, our heavenly Father, who of thy tender mercy didst give thine only Son Jesus Christ to suffer death upon the cross for our redemption; who made there (by his one oblation of himself once offered) a full, perfect and sufficient sacrifice, oblation and satisfaction for the sins of the whole world; and did institute, and in his holy gospel command us to continue, a perpetual memory of that his precious death, until his coming again:

Hear us, O merciful Father, we most humbly beseech thee; and grant that we receiving these thy creatures of bread and wine, according to thy Son our Saviour Jesus Christ's holy institution, in remembrance of his death and passion, may be partakers of his most blessed body and blood:

who, in the same night that he was betrayed, took bread;

Here the priest is to take the paten.

and, when he had given thanks, he brake it,

Here the priest shall break the bread.

and gave it to his disciples, saying, Take, eat;

Here the priest is to lay a hand on all the bread.

this is my body which is given for you:
do this in remembrance of me.
Likewise after supper he took the cup;

Here the priest is to take the cup.

and, when he had given thanks, he gave it to them, saying,
Drink ye all of this;

*Here the priest is to lay a hand on every vessel
in which there is wine to be consecrated.*

for this is my blood of the new testament,
which is shed for you and for many for the remission of sins:
do this, as oft as ye shall drink it, in remembrance of me.

All **Amen.**

The following may be used

All **O Lamb of God**
that takest away the sins of the world,
have mercy upon us.

O Lamb of God
that takest away the sins of the world,
have mercy upon us.

O Lamb of God
that takest away the sins of the world,
grant us thy peace.

Giving of Communion

The priest and people receive communion. To each is said

The body of our Lord Jesus Christ, which was given for thee,
preserve thy body and soul unto everlasting life.
Take and eat this in remembrance that Christ died for thee,
and feed on him in thy heart by faith with thanksgiving.

The blood of our Lord Jesus Christ, which was shed for thee,
preserve thy body and soul unto everlasting life.
Drink this in remembrance that Christ's blood was shed for thee,
    and be thankful.

*Or, when occasion requires, these words may be said once to each row
of communicants, or to a convenient number within each row.*

*If either or both of the consecrated elements are likely to prove
insufficient, the priest returns to the holy table and adds more,
saying the words on page 296 in* Common Worship: Services
and Prayers for the Church of England.

*What remains of the consecrated bread and wine which is not required
for purposes of communion is consumed now or at the end of the
service.*

The Lord's Prayer

The priest may say

As our Saviour Christ hath commanded and taught us,
we are bold to say

All **Our Father, which art in heaven,**
hallowed be thy name;
thy kingdom come;
thy will be done,
in earth as it is in heaven.
Give us this day our daily bread.
And forgive us our trespasses,
as we forgive them that trespass against us.
And lead us not into temptation;
but deliver us from evil.
For thine is the kingdom,
the power and the glory,
for ever and ever.
Amen.

Prayer after Communion

The priest says either the Prayer of Oblation or the Prayer of Thanksgiving.

Prayer of Oblation

O Lord and heavenly Father, we thy humble servants entirely desire thy fatherly goodness mercifully to accept this our sacrifice of praise and thanksgiving; most humbly beseeching thee to grant, that by the merits and death of thy Son Jesus Christ, and through faith in his blood, we and all thy whole Church may obtain remission of our sins, and all other benefits of his passion. And here we offer and present unto thee, O Lord, ourselves, our souls and bodies, to be a reasonable, holy and lively sacrifice unto thee; humbly beseeching thee, that all we, who are partakers of this holy communion, may be fulfilled with thy grace and heavenly benediction. And although we be unworthy, through our manifold sins, to offer unto thee any sacrifice, yet we beseech thee to accept this our bounden duty and service; not weighing our merits, but pardoning our offences, through Jesus Christ our Lord; by whom, and with whom, in the unity of the Holy Ghost, all honour and glory be unto thee, O Father almighty, world without end.

All **Amen.**

Prayer of Thanksgiving

Almighty and ever-living God, we most heartily thank thee, for that thou dost vouchsafe to feed us, who have duly received these holy mysteries, with the spiritual food of the most precious body and blood of thy Son our Saviour Jesus Christ; and dost assure us thereby of thy favour and goodness towards us; and that we are very members incorporate in the mystical body of thy Son, which is the blessed company of all faithful people; and are also heirs through hope of thy everlasting kingdom, by the merits of the most precious death and passion of thy dear Son. And we most humbly beseech thee, O heavenly Father, so to assist us with thy grace, that we may continue in that holy fellowship, and do all such good works as thou hast prepared for us to walk in; through Jesus Christ our Lord, to whom, with thee and the Holy Ghost, be all honour and glory, world without end.

All **Amen.**

Gloria in Excelsis

All   **Glory be to God on high,**
and in earth peace, good will towards men.

We praise thee, we bless thee,
we worship thee, we glorify thee,
we give thanks to thee for thy great glory,
O Lord God, heavenly King,
God the Father almighty.

O Lord, the only-begotten Son Jesu Christ;
O Lord God, Lamb of God, Son of the Father,
that takest away the sins of the world,
have mercy upon us.
Thou that takest away the sins of the world,
have mercy upon us.
Thou that takest away the sins of the world,
receive our prayer.
Thou that sittest at the right hand of God the Father,
have mercy upon us.

For thou only art holy;
thou only art the Lord;
thou only, O Christ,
with the Holy Ghost,
art most high
in the glory of God the Father.
Amen.

The Blessing

The priest says

The peace of God, which passeth all understanding, keep your hearts and minds in the knowledge and love of God, and of his Son Jesus Christ our Lord: and the blessing of God almighty, the Father, the Son, and the Holy Ghost, be amongst you and remain with you always.

All   **Amen.**

A hymn may be sung.

Third Exhortation from
The Book of Common Prayer

Dearly beloved in the Lord, ye that mind to come to the holy Communion of the Body and Blood of our Saviour Christ, must consider how Saint Paul exhorteth all persons diligently to try and examine themselves, before they presume to eat of that Bread, and drink of that Cup. For as the benefit is great, if with a true penitent heart and lively faith we receive that holy Sacrament; (for then we spiritually eat the flesh of Christ and drink his blood; then we dwell in Christ, and Christ in us; we are one with Christ, and Christ with us;) so is the danger great, if we receive the same unworthily. For then we are guilty of the Body and Blood of Christ our Saviour; we eat and drink our own damnation, not considering the Lord's Body; we kindle God's wrath against us; we provoke him to plague us with divers diseases, and sundry kinds of death. Judge therefore yourselves, brethren, that ye be not judged of the Lord; repent you truly for your sins past; have a lively and steadfast faith in Christ our Saviour; amend your lives, and be in perfect charity with all men; so shall ye be meet partakers of those holy mysteries. And above all things ye must give most humble and hearty thanks to God, the Father, the Son and the Holy Ghost, for the redemption of the world by the death and passion of our Saviour Christ, both God and man; who did humble himself, even to the death upon the Cross, for us miserable sinners, who lay in darkness and the shadow of death; that he might make us the children of God, and exalt us to everlasting life. And to the end that we should always remember the exceeding great love of our Master and only Saviour Jesus Christ, thus dying for us, and the innumerable benefits which by his precious blood-shedding he hath obtained to us; he hath instituted and ordained holy mysteries, as pledges of his love, and for a continual remembrance of his death, to our great and endless comfort. To him, therefore, with the Father and the Holy Ghost, let us give (as we are most bounden) continual thanks; submitting ourselves wholly to his holy will and pleasure, and studying to serve him in true holiness and righteousness all the days of our life.

All   **Amen.**

Proper Prefaces from
The Book of Common Prayer

For additional Prefaces, see Note 28 and texts on pages 300–329 in
Common Worship: Services and Prayers for the Church of England.

Christmas

Because thou didst give Jesus Christ thine only Son to be born
as at this time for us; who, by the operation of the Holy Ghost,
was made very man of the substance of the Virgin Mary his mother;
and that without spot of sin, to make us clean from all sin.
Therefore with angels …

Easter

But chiefly are we bound to praise thee for the glorious resurrection
of thy Son Jesus Christ our Lord: for he is the very paschal lamb,
which was offered for us, and hath taken away the sin of the world;
who by his death hath destroyed death, and by his rising to life again
hath restored to us everlasting life.
Therefore with angels …

Ascension

Through thy most dearly beloved Son Jesus Christ our Lord;
who after his most glorious resurrection manifestly appeared to all
his apostles, and in their sight ascended up into heaven to prepare
a place for us; that where he is, thither we might also ascend, and
reign with him in glory.
Therefore with angels …

Pentecost (Whitsun)

Through Jesus Christ our Lord; according to whose most true
promise, the Holy Ghost came down as at this time from heaven
with a sudden great sound, as it might have been a mighty wind,
in the likeness of fiery tongues, lighting upon the apostles, to teach
them, and to lead them to all truth; giving them both the gift of
divers languages, and also boldness with fervent zeal constantly to
preach the gospel unto all nations; whereby we have been brought
out of darkness and error into the clear light and true knowledge
of thee, and of thy Son Jesus Christ.
Therefore with angels …

Who art one God, one Lord; not one only Person, but three Persons in one Substance. For that which we believe of the glory of the Father, the same we believe of the Son, and of the Holy Ghost, without any difference or inequality.
Therefore with angels …

When this Preface is used, the words 'holy Father' must be omitted in the preceding paragraph.

¶ A Collect for the Queen

Almighty and everlasting God,
we are taught by thy holy Word,
    that the hearts of kings are in thy rule and governance,
and that thou dost dispose and turn them
    as it seemeth best to thy godly wisdom:
we humbly beseech thee so to dispose and govern the heart of
    Elizabeth thy Servant, our *Queen* and Governor,
that, in all her thoughts, words, and works,
she may ever seek thy honour and glory,
and study to preserve thy people committed to her charge,
    in wealth, peace, and godliness:
grant this, O merciful Father, for thy dear Son's sake,
    Jesus Christ our Lord.

All **Amen.**

Notes

Notes 1 to 23 apply primarily to Order One.
They are included here insofar as they apply to Order Two.
Notes 24 to 29 apply to Order Two only.

1 **Posture**
   Local custom may be followed and developed in relation to posture. The people should stand for the reading of the Gospel and for the Creed. See also Note 24.

2 **Traditional Texts**
   In addition to the places where they are printed in the service, traditional versions of texts may be used.

3 **Hymns, Psalms, Canticles, the Collection and Presentation of the Offerings of the People, and the Preparation of the Table**
   Points are indicated for these, but they may occur elsewhere.

4 **Sentences**
   Sentences of Scripture appropriate to the season and the place in the service may be used (from Easter Day to Pentecost 'Alleluia' is appropriately added to such sentences).

5 **Acclamations**
   Acclamations, which may include congregational response (such as 'Christ is risen: he is risen indeed') may be used at appropriate points in the service (with 'Alleluia' except in Lent). Acclamations for use before the Gospel are provided on pages 280 and 300–329 in *Common Worship: Services and Prayers for the Church of England*.

6 **Entry**
   At the entry of the ministers, a Bible or Book of the Gospels may be carried into the assembly.

7   **Greetings**
In addition to the points where greetings are provided, at other suitable points (e.g. before the Gospel and before the blessing or dismissal), the greeting 'The Lord be with you' with its response 'and with thy spirit' may be used.

8   **Silence**
Silence is particularly appropriate within the Prayers of Penitence and of Intercession, before the Collect, in response to the reading of the Scriptures, after the Eucharistic Prayer and after the distribution.

9   **Notices**
Banns of marriage and other notices may be published before the service (if possible by a minister other than the president) or before the Prayers of Intercession.

10   **The Prayers of Penitence**
This Note does not apply to Order Two.

11   **The Gloria in Excelsis**
See Note 29.

12   **The Readings**
The readings at Holy Communion are governed by authorized lectionary provision and are not a matter for local decision except where that provision permits.
    Whenever possible, all three readings are used at Holy Communion on Sundays. When only two are read, the minister should ensure that, in any year, a balance is maintained between readings from the Old and New Testaments in the choice of the first reading. The psalm provided relates to the first reading in the lectionary. Where possible it should be used after that reading.

13   **The Sermon**
The sermon is an integral part of the Liturgy of the Word. A sermon should normally be preached at all celebrations on Sundays and Principal Holy Days.
    The sermon may on occasion include less formal exposition of Scripture, the use of drama, interviews, discussion and audio-visual aids.

14   **The Creed**
      The Creed may be preceded by the president saying 'Let us declare
      our faith in God, Father, Son and Holy Spirit'.

15   **The Prayers of Intercession**
      Intercession frequently arises out of thanksgiving; nevertheless these
      prayers are primarily prayers of intercession. They are normally
      broadly based, expressing a concern for the whole of God's world
      and the ministry of the whole Church.
           Prayer for the nation is properly focused in prayer for the
      sovereign by name, and prayer for the Church in prayer for the
      bishop of the diocese by name.
           See also Note 25.

16   **The Peace**
      This Note does not apply to Order Two, but see Note 27.

17   **The Taking**
      In Holy Communion the Church, following the example of the Lord,
      takes, gives thanks, breaks and gives. The bread and wine must be
      taken into the president's hands and replaced upon the table.
      See the rubrics in the Prayer of Consecration (page 13).

18   **The Eucharistic Prefaces**
      When the short Prefaces given on pages 300–329 in *Common
      Worship: Services and Prayers for the Church of England* are used with
      Order Two the phrase 'through Jesus Christ our Lord' must be
      inserted.

19   **The Lord's Prayer**
      On any occasion when the text of an alternative service authorized
      under the provisions of Canon B 2 provides for the Lord's Prayer to
      be said or sung, it may be used in the form included in *The Book of
      Common Prayer* or in either of the two other forms included in
      services in *Common Worship*. The text included in Prayers for Various
      Occasions (page 106 in *Common Worship: Services and Prayers for the
      Church of England*) may be used on suitable occasions.

20   **Breaking of the Bread**
      This Note does not apply to Order Two. See the rubric in the
      Prayer of Consecration (page 13) and Note 27.

21   **Non-communicants**
      At the distribution, any of those distributing the sacrament,
      ordained or lay, may pray for any non-communicants who come
      forward in these or other suitable words: 'May God be with you'
      or 'May God bless you'.

22   **Prayers after Communion**
      This Note does not apply to Order Two.

23   **A Service without Communion**
      When there is no communion, the minister leads the service as far
      as the Prayers of Intercession, and then adds the Lord's Prayer, the
      General Thanksgiving, and/or other prayers, ending with the Grace.

The following notes apply to Order Two only

Frequently used additions to the text of The Book of Common Prayer
are included in Order Two but are indented from the left hand margin.

24   **Posture**
      It is appropriate for the people to kneel for the opening prayer
      and Commandments, the Prayers of Intercession, the confession,
      absolution and Comfortable Words, the Prayer of Consecration
      and prayers after the distribution.

25   **Supplementary Material**
      Supplementary Texts may be used with Order Two when they are
      compatible with that Order. The third form of intercession in the
      Supplementary Texts (page 283 in *Common Worship: Services and
      Prayers for the Church of England*) may be used in place of the
      form printed.

26   **The Sermon**
      At the discretion of the priest, the sermon may precede the Creed.

27   **Alternative Order**
Where customary, the Prayer of Humble Access may precede
'Lift up your hearts'; 'Amen' may be omitted at the end of the Prayer
of Consecration, and the Prayer of Oblation follow immediately;
the Lord's Prayer may follow the Prayer of Oblation; the versicle
'The peace of the Lord be always with you' with the response
'And with thy spirit' may follow the Lord's Prayer and precede the
Agnus Dei. In Order Two, but not in Order Two in Contemporary
Language, the breaking of the bread may be deferred until the
Agnus Dei.

28   **Proper Prefaces**
The short Proper Prefaces in the Seasonal Provisions (pages
300–329 in *Common Worship: Services and Prayers for the Church of
England*) may be used with Order Two. In such case the priest
inserts the words 'through Jesus Christ our Lord' after 'almighty,
everlasting God'. The texts of the Proper Prefaces from *The Book of
Common Prayer* for use with Order Two are given on pages 18–19.

29   **The Gloria in Excelsis**
If the Gloria in excelsis is not to be used on every occasion,
it is appropriately omitted on Sundays in Advent and Lent and
on all weekdays that are not Principal Holy Days or Festivals.

General Rules for Regulating Authorized Forms of Service

1. Any reference in authorized provision to the use of hymns shall be construed as including the use of texts described as songs, chants, canticles.

2. If occasion requires, hymns may be sung at points other than those indicated in particular forms of service. Silence may be kept at points other than those indicated in particular forms of service.

3. Where rubrics indicate that a text is to be 'said' this must be understood to include 'or sung' and vice versa.

4. Where parts of a service make use of well-known and traditional texts, other translations or versions, particularly when used in musical compositions, may be used.

5. Local custom may be established and followed in respect of posture but regard should be had to indications in Notes attached to authorized forms of service that a particular posture is appropriate for some parts of that form of service.

6. On any occasion when the text of an alternative service authorized under the provisions of Canon B 2 provides for the Lord's Prayer to be said or sung, it may be used in the form included in *The Book of Common Prayer* or in either of the two other forms included in services in *Common Worship*. The further text included in Prayers for Various Occasions (page 106 in *Common Worship: Services and Prayers for the Church of England*) may be used on suitable occasions.

7. Normally on any occasion only one Collect is used.

8. At Baptisms, Confirmations, Ordinations and Marriages which take place on Principal Feasts, other Principal Holy Days and on Sundays of Advent, Lent and Easter, within the Celebration of the Holy Communion, the Readings of the day are used and the Collect of the Day is said, unless the bishop directs otherwise.

9. The Collects and Lectionary in *Common Worship* may, optionally, be used in conjunction with the days included in the Calendar of *The Book of Common Prayer*, notwithstanding any difference in the title or name of a Sunday, Holy Day or other observance included in both Calendars.

Authorization

The texts contained in this booklet are authorized pursuant to Canon B 2 of the Canons of the Church of England for use until further resolution of the General Synod.

Acknowledgements

The publisher gratefully acknowledges permission to reproduce copyright material in this book.

Published sources include the following:

The Archbishops' Council of the Church of England: *The Prayer Book as Proposed in 1928*, which is copyright © The Archbishops' Council of the Church of England.

Cambridge University Press: Extracts (and adapted extracts) from *The Book of Common Prayer*, the rights in which are vested in the Crown, are reproduced by permission of the Crown's Patentee, Cambridge University Press.